CO

DICTIONARY OF

METAPHORS &
SIMILES

V&S PUBLISHERS

Published by:

F-2/16, Ansari Road, Daryaganj, New Delhi-110002
011-23240026, 011-23240027 • *Fax:* 011-23240028
Email: info@vspublishers.com • *Website:* www.vspublishers.com

Regional Offi ce : Hyderabad
5-1-707/1, Brij Bhawan (Beside Central Bank of India Lane)
Bank Street, Koti, Hyderabad - 500 095
040-24737290
E-mail: vspublishershyd@gmail.com

Branch Offi ce : Mumbai
Flat No. Ground Floor, Sonmegh Building
No. 51, Karel Wadi, Thakurdwar, Mumbai - 400 002
022-22098268
E-mail: vspublishersmum@gmail.com

Follow us on:

For any assistance sms **VSPUB** to **56161**
All books available at **www.vspublishers.com**

© **Copyright:** *V&S Publishers*
ISBN 978-93-505714-8-4
Edition 2014

Printed at : Param Offseters Okhla New Delhi-110020

Publisher's Note

A simile is where two things are directly compared because they share a common feature. The word *as* or *like* is used to compare the two words. For example, *as* cold *as* a dog's nose. The clouds were *as* fluffy *as* cotton wool. The clouds were fluffy like cotton wool. A simile is only one of dozens of specific types of metaphor. In short, a simile is a type of metaphor in which the comparison is made with the use of the word *like or its equivalent*: My love is like a red, red rose.

Considering the growing importance of English in all spheres of life, we recently published an EXC-EL Series (Excellence in English Language) composed of four books - English Vocabulary Made Easy, English Grammar & Usage, Spoken English, and Improve Your Vocabulary. We thought we have done our bit. No sooner, the Series hit the market; a volley of readers sought our help to improve diction, presentation and attractiveness of their conversation – both in writing and speaking.

Being aware that our existence as a publishing house depends solely upon fulfilling readers' expectations and continued patronage, we decided to come out with something that can add spark to any conversation while making it appear interesting. This Dictionary of Metaphors & Similes is the outcome. There are three more companion dictionaries on – Idioms, Phrases and Proverbs..

This book explains the meaning behind hundreds of Metaphors & Similes that you hear or read in English each day. *The meanings are shown in italics.* In order to keep it concise, this dictionary attempts to present most commonly used Metaphors & Similes. Having an exhaustive one will just overwhelm you with thousands of Metaphors & Similes that nobody uses anymore. English remains immensely popular, attractive, articulate and rich language but the confusion between Metaphors & Similes is sometimes 'tough nuts to crack'.

What led us to publish this? Metaphors & Similes appear in every language, and English has thousands of them. They are often confusing. In order to understand a language, you must know the precise meaning of metaphor and simile in that language mean. Unless you know the underlying difference between the two, you will get completely befuddled.

We would be happy to have your views and comments for improving the content and quality of the edition.

METAPHORS

Introduction Metaphors

What are Metaphors?

A metaphor is a figure of speech that describes a subject by asserting that it is, on some point of comparison, the same as another otherwise unrelated object. Metaphor is a type of analogy and is closely related to other rhetorical figures of speech that achieve their effects via association, comparison or resemblance including allegory, hyperbole, and simile.

In simpler terms, a metaphor compares two objects or things without using the words "like" or "as". One of the most prominent examples of a metaphor in English literature is the All the world's a stage monologue from As You Like It:

Following is a list of Metaphors with their Meanings. Read, understand and learn them as they may be of great help in your day to day conversations and in making sentences as well as in writing good English.

A

800 lb gorilla
A powerful organization that runs without paying heed to rules and laws.

A battle
Referring to something that may

A beacon for fellow workers
A

A

A classroom
Somewhere where one learns, and

A cleanskin
A

reputation

A david and goliath battle
A struggle between two parties who

A game
A

life.

A gem is not polished without rubbing

A Herculean cleaning of the stables
A thorough revision of operating

A kick in the shins
A

(To be a) Moose
R

A Roland for an Oliver
Tit for tat.

A stab in the dark
A sheer guess

A stiff upper lip
O
pain or adversioty

A stitch in time saves nine

A tale out of fruit-cake land

fairy-tale.

A tidal wave of (something)
An overwhelming manifestation

an overwhelming manifestation of some emotion or phenomenon.

Abandon ship
T

Above one's head

(To be) Abrasive
Rough/ hurtful.
A
T
(To be) Adrift
Wandering.
(To be an) Airhead
T
or a stupid person.
(An) Albatross
An emotional burden.
A
Fully prepared.
All he touches turns to gold!
R
(After the story of Midas whose thoughtless request that whatever

granted by Dionysus.)
All hell broke loose
G
All systems go
T
possible.
All-embracing
T
Am whacked!
Exhausted.
America is a melting pot
Culturally diverse.
An Aladdin's cave
A

An ass in a lion's skin

An epic
A
An iron anvil should have a hammer of feathers

and gentleness.
An old lover.
An urchin
S
Angel
To be very good-natured.
Appeal from philip drunk to philip sober
Wait to return to normality.
Apple of my eye
To be the most adored person to someone.
Apple-polishing
T

(To be) Arcadian
Rural and simple.
Argus-eyed
W
Asleep at the switch
Inattentive.
Assembly-line justice

At a loose end

At crossroads
A

At the beginning.

Personally.
At full throttle
Using all your efforts, energies.
At white heat
Of intense passion.
Aunt Sally
Used when referring to a target

Authority is a chair, it needs legs to stand up
Authority requires the support of people.
Away with the fairies
O
sufferers from senile dementia.

B

Back to the drawing board!

Bad bobbin
To be the worst.

(To be) Bait
L

Ball the jack

everything on one try.

Bang/knock their heads together
Bring sense by means of mutual

Barn-burner
Destroyer.

Be a heckle to

Be a recipe for (disaster/happiness/success etc)
I

Be all thumbs

Be born/come on the wrong side of the blanket
Be bastard-born.

Be in disharmony
Refers to quarrelling.

Be on the right rail

Be run down

Be two folk
Be unfriendly.

Be wound up

Bear the palm

Bear's service

more harm than good.

Bed of nails
P

Bed of roses
Something that is very pleasant and easy.

Before the ink is dry
Immediately.

Beg like a cripple at a cross/on a bridge
With great importunity.

Beggars can't be choosers

Begin/lead the dance

Being cold as ice
  Very severe.
  Belling the cat
  T
Bend the bow of Ulysses
  T
  man.
Better to wear out than rust out

B

Between hammer and anvil
  Between two equally devastating evils.
(Am) Bewitched

Big red button
  For the purpose of starting something.
Big wheel
  An important person.
Billy has found a pin

Binding
  T
Bird of ill omen
  A person with a reputation of

Bird's-eye maple

  woman
Birth-control hours

  one spouse sleeping by day and the other at night.

B

Bitter truth
  Harsh truth.
Bittersweet memories
  Good and bad memories.
Black magic
  E
(To be) Black
  To be impure, evil.
Black-hearted
  T
Blacksmith's daughter

Blizzard of activity
  S
Blot on the landscape
  An intruder or intrusion that spoils otherwise pleasing surroundings.
Blot out
  Annihilate.
Blow a gasket/fuse

Blow hot and cold

Blow hot and cold
  T
Blow your boiler
  Lose your temper.
Blow/let off steam
  Release surplus energy, suppressed

Blowed in the glass
  Genuine .
Blown away
  T

Blue as wad Long
  Standing but irr

Blue in the face
To be upset.
Blue skies
Signify happiness.
Bluebeard

Bluebeard's key

Boil not the pap before the child is born

required.
Boil
T
swell.
Boiling frog
R

Boiling mad
Very angry.
Boiling landscape

as a liquid. Time is an essential

Bolt from the blue
A
Bond
T
Bookworm

Borrowed plumes

as their own.
Bosom friend
R
in bra.
Bottom feeder
A person who lives a very lowly life, barely surviving.

Bottom out

before an upturn.
Bound to
Fated to do something.
Brain-child

thought, ideas.
Brass ring
Living life to the fullest.
Bread and circuses
S
the population at the expense of

B
T

Break his horn-book

Break the mould
T
Break the sound-barrier

Break the thread

Break
To end something.
Breaking news.

B
Filled with anger, inside and out.
Bright mind
Intelligent, smart.
Brilliant idea
A really good idea.
Broken heart

sad.

Brought the pack to the pins
Dwindled away the goods.

Brought up to speed
Prepared for entry into a gang.

Brownie points

Bubbly personality
To be full of energy, very high-

Bubbly personality
E

Bucket brigade
A method of moving items by passing those items from one

Bucking for a raise

Buffer state
Country situated between two possible enemy states.

Bugbear
Needless fear.

Buridan's ass

Burn-out

Burst his boiler
Come or bring to grief.

Burst
T

Taste is territorial, and strong

Bury your head in the sand

Butt-shut

By one and one spindles are made

C

Cadmean victory

loss.

Caged emotions
Feeling boxed in, full of hatred

Camel's nose
P

Carry the seeds of change

Carry weight of the world
To appear or behave as if burdened by all the problems in the whole world

Carry weight
T

Case-harden

Cassandra

Cast in mould

Cast in someone's mould
M

Casten in a calm
Neat.

Cast-iron

Cat's paw

Cease the day
T
that are provided in life.

Chapter of accidents
Refers to a series of unforeseen events.

Character assassination
D

Chase the rainbow
Pursue an ideal, illusion. (From

Cheek by jowl

Chicken out of
Abandon

Chill out!

down.

Chilly
U

Chimerical

Chinese puzzle
A perplexing enigma.

Chink in someone's armour
A

not be done.
Chink of light
A small hope of a solution or

Chip in
T
Circuit-breaker

a dispute.
Clam up
T
Clamp down on

Clean sweep

Clean up a mess
T
Clean up one;s act
T
affairs.
Clear skies
Devoid of danger.
Clear-cut

Clip someone's wings
A

Closed book
T
Coarse (about or with something/ one)
R
Cock and bull story
An improbable tale.
Cockatrice egg
Starting point of deadly danger.

Cog in the machine

identity.
Cold feet
To be nervous.
C
To be an unemotional person.
Collide
T
Colorful remark
A
Come alive to

Come apart at the seams
T
Come back to haunt someone
T
person.
Come clean
T
Come down on someone like a hammer

Come down with a thud
To be suddenly disillusioned.
Come home
Be born.
Come out into the open

Come out of the closet
T
Come past the smithy

Come through loud and clear
To be well understood.
Come to life
Fully realised.
Come unstuck/unglued

fail.

17

Conjecture

Consumed by love
Filled with love.
Cool

Copper-bottom

Copper-hearted
Untrustworthy.
Core-dump on
Complain, explain fully to, pour

Couch potato
A very lazy person.
Countdown has started

Court disaster
To do something that will be harmful to onself.
Crab-apple
T
behaviour.
Crank up

Crazy/silly as a two-bob watch
Completely mad.
Crocodile tears

Crocodiles' teeth are white daggers
C

Cross one's mind
T
something

Crucible period

Cry for the moon
Demand the impossible, the unattainable.
Cry out for
Demand vehemently, imperiously,

Cry wolf

false alarms.
Cuckoo
T
Cuff ears

Cultural mosaic

Cut blocks with a razor
Waste talents.
Cut down to size

Cut off at the web's end
Finished before time.
Cut your teeth

Cute as a wooden box

wooden box is thought of as a

D

Dance attendance
Wait obsequiously, assiduously on another.

Dance barnaby

haste.

Dance to someone else's pipe/tune/whistle

lead.

Dance/march to a different tune

Daniel come to judgement
T
wisdom.

Darby and Joan

Dark horse
A

Dead duck
To have failed, or to be in a hopeless situation.

Dead in the water

Dead tired
To be extremely tired.

Deaf as a nail
Hard/right [straight]/sure as nails.

Deep dark secret
A

Deep despair
Lot of sadness.

Deep, dark thoughts
S

Diamond in the rough
A person who is good natured but

Did he fall or was he pushed?

they seem.

Dim view
A very narrow viewpoint.

Dinosaur
Someone who is very old.

Dip one's pen in gall
To write with bitterness.

Dipped in the Shannon
Not in the least bashful.

(To be a) Dodo
A fool.
Doesn't know yet he's been born

world.
Dog in the manger

someone prevents another having what he needs, although he does not want it himself.
Dog one's trail
To follow.
Dog-eared pages
P
folded over a long time.
Dog-tired
To be very tired.
Don't fall before you're pushed

Don't let your imagination run away with you
One should not mix fantasy with reality.
Don't lift me till I fall

Don't take the axe out of the carpenter's hand

wherewithal.
Done and dusted

Don't bite off more than you can chew
O

Dot the i's
Go into detail.
Down on all fours

Down the line

Drag one's feet
Delay deliberately.
Draw a picture

Draw the king's/queen's picture

Drive it home
Ensure full understanding.
Drive not a second nail until the

Finish one job before starting another.
Drive the nail home/to the head

Drive the nail where it will go

possible.
Driving force

Drop into the lap of

Drop/dump/throw in the lap of

burden to.
Drop/throw off the mask
Reveal yourself in your true er.

Dry spell

Shortage of something.

Dry straight

survive a testing time.

Dry-nurse

appointed to do so.

Duck-hover

Dying to

E

Earn his/her wings as

Easy targets over which trainee

bombing runs.

Eat dog for another
Oblige.

Eat well of the cresses
Be sure to remember.

Eat-the-pack
Spendthrift.

Education is a gateway to success
E

Electrify
To Startle.

Elephant in the room
R

is still ignored.

Eleven cuts to the hank

Embark
To begin.

Enchant

End of story! Really, that is all there is to be said about it.

information that needs no further explanation.

End on a sour note
Ending something badly.

Endowed with
To be gifted naturally.

End-product
Final form

Espouse/embrace
T

Even steaming!

of the other.

Every jewel needs a setting
A beautiful woman, unpartnered, is wasted.

Every pedlar must carry his own pack

only do for yourself.

Every pedlar praises his own pack

   endation.

Every schoolboy knows that!

(To) Exist

   To be.

Eyes peeled

     something Life is a dream Life is

F

Face like a bagful of spanners
  Rough and lumpy.
Face like a smacked arse!
  Feeling sorry for oneself.
Face like a smith's anvil
  Hard and unyielding.
Face like a welder's bench
  Disagreeable.
Face of brass/brassy/brazen:
  Impudently bold.
Face the music
  F
Fade off to sleep

  go to sleep.
Fail to see (your) logic

Fairy godfather

Fairy godmother

Fairy story!

F

  grief, fail utterly.

Fall to the ground

  abandoned.
Fast as a rivet

(To) Father

Feed into

Feeling blue
  Feeling sad.
Feeling rough
  Not feeling well.
Fell the web
  Finish off.
Find a false prophet
  Be disappointed by someone.
Find a horse-nest
  Laugh without reason.
Find a mare's nest

  that you imagine to be important.
Fine-drawn
  Exaggerated.
Finish Aladdin's window

  genius.

Fire is day, when it goes out it's night
Fire brightens the surroundings,

left.
Fishing for something

Fits to a T

Flash-point

Flaxen Pale

Flirt with an idea
To give something little amount

attention.
Flogging a dead horse
Wasting time on something even though its fate has already been

Fly on the wheel

has not done.
Fly-by-night

disappear overnight.

Fly-by-sky
Flighty, imaginative, volatile, unsteady person.
(To) Foil
Someone or something juxtaposed

For want of a nail
Attention to detail is important.
Force of a steam hammer

Force someone's hand
T

Forge
Create something strong and durable.
Fork in the road

Four Asian Tigers
Referring to the highly developed

Taiwan, South Korea and Hong Kong.
From the same smithy

Frozen with fear
T
to move.
Full blooded

G

Gain the upper hand
To attain, after some effort, an advantage over another person.

Galvanise

Gamut the complete range or scope of something
The whole gamut of human emotion

Gas-bag

Gather up the threads/pull the threads together

orderly interrelationship.

Geared to

on.

Get a foot/a toe in the door
Gain entry

Get a hair in one's neck

Get a head of steam behind...
Obtain powerful support or

Get close to the bone
T

Get down to brass tacks

Get off the ground

Get one's lug in the loof
Severely dealt with.

Get one's screw out

Get out of one's pram

Get round a man's neck-hole
T

Get steam up/get up steam

Get the lease
Understand rightly.

Get the lion's share
Get the largest share.

Get the picture
Have enough information to understand the situation.

Get under feet

Get weaving
To start.

Get cold feet

Get/take the steel out of...
Get the best out of something or someone.

Giant-killer

large organisation.

Gimlet-eyed
Keen-eyed, given to peering into things.

Gipsy's warning
A dangerous warning.

Gipsy-legged

Give (someone) the cold shoulder
To show that one is unwilling to be friendly with (a person)

Give a handle to...

G
To pay dues.

Give birth to...

Give full marks for
G

Give her rock another tow

of.

Give him room to grow
G

Give pap with a hatchet

Give someone the cold shoulder
Ostentaniously to ignore a person

Glowing review
A good review.

Glued to
Closely applied to.

Glued-on
Added haphazardly without being integrated with the main part of

Glued-up
Assembled at random.

Go against the grain

G
As fast as possible

Go begging
Be available for anyone who wants it.

Go for the doctor

Go hand in hand
To be inseparable.

Go home and kick the dog
T

G

Go into orbit

Go into rhapsodies
Enthuse extravagantly.

Go into your dance

Go nthrough something with a

T
investigation

Go on an overdrive
Over-response.

Go on shirt-buttons

Go over his mother's thumb

Go pear-shaped
Go wrong, amiss.
Go round by Robin Hood's barn

Go the whole hog
Do something without reservation

G

G
Without food or money.
Go/run off the rails/track

have an extramarital affair.
Gobsmacked
Surprised and astounded.
Going on like Sokespitch's can

Grate on
Annoy.
G
Bribe.
Grease/oil the wheels

Great engines turn on a little pin
An unimportant person may have

organisation.
Great weights hang on thin wires

persons may be the instruments of great events.
Greek gift
O

Green light
S
ahead.
(To be) Green
To be new or inelegant or immature.
(A) Greenie
A
Grey area
Neither this nor that in a situation.
Grey skies
Referring to bad times.
(To) Grill
To question.
Grind to a halt
Stop slowly but inevitably.
Grit in the oil

Gun with no bullets
S
useless for the desired purpose.

Hag knots

Hag ridden harassed
Oppressed in mind (as if ridden by

Hag's teeth
Protruding lumps of matting.
Hail of bullets
Hard and driven
Hair by hair you will pull out the horse's tail

Halting speech

Ham
Someone who shows off.
Hammer and pincers/pinsons

H
Punish.
Hammer it out

(To) Hammer

Hammer-and-tongs/-pinsons

R   *during*

Handle to his name
A title.
Handpick someone
T

Handy as a gimlet

Hang by a thread

Hang together (in/on a string)

Hang upon the skirts of

far from them.
Hanging over one's head
Refers to An imminent misfortune.
Hard-bitten
T
Hard-boiled
T
Hard-wired

emerge with maturation rather than

Harmony
Referring to good understanding.
(To) Harness
T

Has a chip on his shoulder
Is annoyed about something.
Has a screw loose

Has cut his eye/wisdom teeth/has all his back teeth

Has his head screwed on right

Has his mother's milk in the nose

Has the gliding angle of a brick

Have a bad/good nail in oneself
being naturally bad/good.
Have a ball
Have fun.
Have a blacksmith's eye

judging.
Have a chip on one's shoulder
Unreasonably to resent something
Have a close shave
T
Have a green thumb
T
Have a heart of stone
T
Have a needle into
Bear a grudge, spite against.
Have a purple heart
To be brave.
Have a rag on every bush
Court many women.
Have a rod in pickle
Be prepared.

Have a ball.
Have a good time
H

Have brass/cast-iron balls
To be foolhardy.
Have many/other irons/heats in the

Keep other possibilities in reserve.
Have no weft in oneself
To have no energy.
Have one hand tied behind one's back
T
Have other tow to tease
Other things to do.
Have over a barrel

Have sour grapes
To be envious.
Have taken one's gears in
To stop doing anything.
Have taken one's reed and gears in
To die.
Have the oil-bottle in your pocket

Have the primrose path
To have an easy life.
Have woven one's piece
T
H
A name playfully applied to

or lets something slip from their

Having (other) tow on one's distaff

Having great taste
T

30

He has a heart
R

He has ink in his pen
Sexually vigorous.
He has no ink in his pen
Brainless.
He is yellow
M
Head of tow
With very fair hair
Heart-of-oak

sterling quality.
Heated debate
A

Heckle her tow

Herculean task
E
Hermetically sealed

off from the outside environment
Hew to the line

Hide one's light under a bushel
T

Hiding behind (a woman's) skirts

Hit the (right) nail on the head

Hit the buffers

Hold a winning hand
To be in an unbeatable position
Hold soemone's hand
To give detailed on-the-job-training and supervision
Hold the baby

responsibility.
Home (in) on...

Homespun

Hooked to

to something/one.
Hug the shore
To be unadventurous.

I

I am charmed by her

I am Engineering a
To Contrive.
I'll give thee bell-tinker
To give one a good thrashing.
I'm talking to the engineer, not
the oily rag
In dismissing an interruption.
Icy stare
A very stern stare.
Ideas are water
Ideas are similar to water in the

are of different forms, are

I'm all thumbs
V

In a cold sweat
To be afraid.
In a groove
In a settled routine.
In a holding pattern

In a hole

In cold blood
Deliberately and unemotionally.

In full blast
In full operation.
In high gear

phase.
In his buttons
Destined.
In its infancy

In long clothes

In more strife than a pork chop in
a synagogue
In an embarrassing situation.
In orbit

exultant.
In the black
T
In the doghouse
T
In the heat of

In the lap of luxury
Living in supreme luxury.
In the loop

sary information.

In the melting-pot

In the red
T
In the throes of

something.
In the wrong box

I
Many possibilities.

Get maddeningly angry
Ink into
Emphasise and set permanently.
Intermesh with

Iron will

Iron-bound coast

dangerous to ships.
It augurs well for

It is as broad as long/as long as broad

way you regard it.
It is Greek to me
Not understandable.
It ought to be scrapped!

It rains by planets
I
It's been a long, bumpy road
A
It's like beating a dead horse
I
It's raining men

J

Judge not a book by its cover
Do not judge someone/thing by

Judgment of Solomon
Using wisdom to bring about

Jump into bed with someone
*To enter into a joint enterprise
with another person*

Jumping for joy
To be very happy.

Jumping the shark
Trying to revive something when it

Jump-start

outside impulse

K

Keep in leading-strings

Keep in the background

Keep someone in the dark
D
uninformed.

Keep the band in the nick
Keep things running smoothly

Keep the oyster
Retain the best part.

Keep the wheel in the nick
Keep on good terms.

Keep your boiler clear!

abdominal) health.

Kick in the pants

Kick off
T

Kick one in Slaidburn and they all limp in Newton

nomine.

Kick someone around
To abuse a person.

Kick the bucket
Die.

Kick the bucket
Died.

Kick the cat
T

Kick the tires

Kill oneself by laughing
To be grtaetly amused

Kill the goose that lays the golden eggs

greed of the moment.

King-pin

Kiss and tell
T

Kiss of death
Something intended to be helpful

Kiss the child for the nurse's sake
Have ulterior motives.

Kiss the dust
T

Kiss the ground
To revere or bless the alnd, or to be overthrouwn.

Kiss the rod

Knap the rust

and leave.
Knock on other doors

Knock/rub the corners off

Knock/rub the corners off

Knock/sing at a deaf man's door

request.
Knock/throw for a loop

Know all the answers
To outwit others.
Kow-tow to...
Admit and submit to an authority.

L

Labour of Hercules

strength.
Labour of Sisyphus/Sisyphean labour
Unending toil.
Lady-killer

Lame duck
A person who has lost.
landslide victory
A
Large as life/life-size

Larger than life
E
Laugh in a sea of sadness
A

Laundry list
A large set of demands
Lay down guide-lines

be followed.
Lay down the law
T
Lay it on the line
T

Lay one's card on the table
T

Lay/spread it on thick/with a trowel

Lay it on the line

‑

Lead one a (pretty) dance

from an admirer.
Lead someone up the gardebn path
Mislead a person by deliberately

Leading question
A
as to suggest the answer
Leaf out
To be slightly retarded.
L

position.
Leap in the dark
A
Leaping with laughter
Laughing a lot.
Leave no stone unturned

Leave others for dead
To be vastly superior.
Leave someone clold
To fail to impress
Left in the basket

Lend a hand
To assist.
Let sleeping dogs lie
To let something (a situation) be as it is.
Let the want come at the web's end

the very last moment.
Lick into shape
Train to a useful or presentable standard
Lie at the door of

Lie for/deserve the whetstone
Be an outrageous liar.
Life is a dream
Life is short and goes by so

Life in the fast lane
A
to live.

shadow on a cloudy day
L
has to end someday.
Life is a shuttle
Life is never uniform.
Life sucks!:

Lift the curtain
To Reveal.
Lift the veil of Isis

Lift your undercarriage
Be off with you! Get going!
Light at the end of the tunnel
A long-awaited improvement in

Light in a sea of darkness
A ray of hope in a very impossible situation.
Lightening rod
A
Lily white
To be pure.
Limp-dick
T
Lint-white
Very white.
Live from hand to mouth
B
Live on the smell of an oil-rag
Refuse to spend money on food.
Live wire
T

Load of rubbish
Blatant nonsense.
Lock antlers with someone
To have an argument with another person.
Lock, stock and barrel
Entirely.
Lone wolf
A
without involving others.
Long arm jurisdiction
To be able to pass a judgement on

situations.
Look after number one
T

Look in the pink
L
Look into the crystal ball

Look to one's laurels

Lose one touch
T
thing/someone
Lose one's nerve
To abandon, out of fear, to do something
Lose one's shirt
M
Lose/run out of steam

to slow down
Lost one's temper-pin

Love is a camera, full of memories
L
a lot of memories.

the warmth of spring
Feeling of love unfolding to the warmth of a lover.
Love is a growing garland
L
day.
Love is a lemon-either bitter or sweet
L

some sweet parts.
Love is a thrill ride
Love is thrilling.
Love is in the air
Love is all around.
Love stinks!
love is the worst feeling.

M

Mad-hatter
T
Make (someone) sit up
Compel to be more alert.
Make (something) stick

proven home.
Make a mental note of...
Remember something that has to be said later.
Make a wheelwright of...

Make causey webs
T
idly.
Make mountains out of molehill
To treat a minor problem as though it were a major disaster
Make one's mark

Make the grade

enough to go forward.
M

Make whim-whams for a goose's bridle

Making a pig of oneself
Demeaning oneself
Man cannot spin and reel at the same time

Man in the moon

Man of iron

Man of one book
T
Marry
To join two things.
Mecca
O
Medusa's head
S
a person.
Melt-down

Mesh with

Miles apart
T

Milk for babies

for the young or ignorant.

Miss on one/four/all cylinder(s)

Misty, water-coloured memories
Vague memories
Misty
D
Money begets money

start with.
Monitor

Monkey paw

Monkey see, monkey do
Trying to learn something without

Monster/ogre/witch
To be bad-natured.
More belongs to marriage than four bare legs in a bed
L
Mother hen
A
Mother of the mine

Mother's milk
An essential, elementary need.
Motherhood stae,ent
A statement so obvious and

Mould on...
Try to imitate.
Mount the ass
T
Mountain climb
A
Mountain of strength
Very strong
(To be an) Mouse
Refers to someone who is timid.
Movable feast
A
a set date
Movbe on to greener pastures
To move to a better environment
Move down a notch
T
Move heaven and earth
To do everything possible
Move the goal posts
Unfairly to alter the rules after

Mudslinging
I

Mutton dressed up as a lamb
Foolishly pretend to be younger

To be madly in love
My memory is a little cloudy

My thread is spun
My life is over.

N

Nail someone
T

Name to conjure with

Neither rhyme nor reason
No sense.
Neither side nor selvedge

Nerves of iron/steel
V

Net
T
Never darken my door again
Do not ever return
New lease of life
P
Nick the thread
Put an end to life.
Nip something in the bud
T
stages when stopping ti is still relatively easy
No room at the inn
N
No way to run a railroad!
A disastrous way to go about anything
Not a penny the better/worse

amount.
Not britched yet

N

Not know one's ABC from a battledore
Illiterate.
Not put a foot wrong

Not to be wortha continental
To have no value
Not to have the foggiest notion
T

Not to lose any sleep over something
Not to worry about some matter
Nothing to make a song about!

Nought but what was put in with a spoon

Nourish a serpent in your bosom

Nourish vain hopes, resentful feelings etc.

them.
Nurse to life

Nurse-tree

Nuts and bolts
B

O

Off the pin of the wheel/the wire
Wandering from the point.
Off-beam/off the beam

Oil the wheel that squeaks
Deal with the demanding ones

Old man of the sea

On a cold day in hell
Never
On a hiding to nothing
Confronted with a hurtful situation

it.
On a learning curve
Trying to master an unfamiliar

On automatic pilot

On cloud nine
Very happy.
On the afternoon turn now!

On the beam

On the blink

On the cards
Possibly.
On the losing end of the stick
To be worse off while the other

On the pulse
T

On the rims

Once removed from a Bozzill
Bad-tempered and restless.
One nail drives out another
Two people performing the same

or trouble dispels another.
One/single track mind

Open sesame

Open the ball

quarrel
Open the pack
Tell the news.

Open your budget

Open your poke and sell your wares
Open your mouth and tell your thoughts, your opinion.
(To be an) Ostrich

Ostrich effect
A

Our marriage is on the rocks
Marriage is going through a

Out of the blue
T
Out of the picture

Owl
A night person
(An) Ox
Refers to a big and strong man.

P,Q

Packet-boys

wind.
Painful lesson in life
A

Paint a black/bleak/gloomy

worst terms.
Paint him in his proper colours

Paint him with his warts/warts and all
Spare no detail
Paint in bright colours

Palmy days
Triumphant and good times.
Paper candidate
A

name on the ballot.
Paper-hearted
To be feeble.
Paper-thin
To be inadequate.
Parthian shot

Pass the hat

P
T

Patch up (something)
Repair
Patched up

Pay the ferryman
T
Peachy
To be pretty.
Pedlar's/tinker's news
Old news.
Peggy with her lantern
Elusive person.
Penelopize
T
Penny soul never comes to twopence
Of natural limitations.
Pick/take up the thread(s)
Resume something previously interrupted.
Pied Piper

away from where they should be.

(A) Pig
T
matters of hygiene.
Piggyback
Assist, subsidise.
Piggyback heart

surgery into a patient whose own heart needs supplementing.
Piggyback rail/car

Pincer movement

Pinchbeck
False, spurious.
Pivotal
Playing an essential part
Planet-struck
E
Plans are still a little hazy
P
Plateau effect

(A) Platform
A

Play one tune and dance another
Say one thing and do another.
Play patty-cake with...

relationship with someone.
Please the pigs

Plug gaps
Fill in gaps.
Podunk

Point of no return

Poison pill
A
its initial purpose.
Polish off
Dispose of.
Polished

Polonian
To be sententious.
Pork barrel legislation or patronage
A

Position
A
Position: One's position on a political issue

Pray to God but keep hammering

Preach to the converted
To say something to those who already believe in it
Press/push the button

Procrustean bed

adhered to.
Procrustean
Imposing a brutal uniformity.
Promethean man

Pull a dead lion's beard off
Exhibit false valour.

46

Pull the chocks away

Pull the pin

Pull the right string
T
Pull your freight
Depart soon or suddenly.
Pull/take the chestnuts out of the

Get someone else to do your

Puppet government
A government manipulated by foreign power.
Push the envelope
Explore, pioneer beyond the point

Put a loop in your life

Put a night on the yarn-winds
To have a boring evening.
Put a ring around that
To be sure of something.
P
Try every means.
Put grit in the machine
Interfere.

Put him in a hole

whom you should be sharing.
Put in the picture
Inform fully.
Put in your clutch
Go quiet.
Put into the crucible
Renew.
Put on hold

Put one's head in a wolf's mouth
T
Put out on the shool/shovel

P
Prepare to do a job.
P
Use little means, plus faith and

ends.
Put your hand up
Confess.
Quicksilver
R
temperament.

R

Race
  A
Rag-bag of Motley

Railroad

  A
Raining cats and dogs
  R
Rain-maker

Rap over the knuckles

Ratchet up/down

  amounts.
Ratchet-mouth

Read him like a book
  Be thoroughly familiar.
Read into

Read on one side of the leaf
  T
  situation.
Ready for Blind Charlie's cart

Reality is an enemy
  *Reality is not as good and easy as
  it is made out to be.*
Reams of...
  Large quantities of...
Recharge the batteries

  energies by rest and other refreshment.
Red ball

  travel fast
Red card
  S

  S
Red shoes syndrome

  and age problems.
Red-line
  D

Red-line
Push to the limit

*mean that there is a literal smell.
Instead, it is just apparent that the*

Reel in
B
Rest on one's laurels
*T
earned in earlier times as a*

Rest on our laurels

Retread
Retrain people for new jobs.
Reverse ferret
T

Reverse the ratchet

Ride the hatch
T
Rider
*S
new to an existing bill.*
Riding coattails
V

Rise from the ashes
Revive, return to normal after

Road Hog
Territorially aggressive driver.
Robin Hood's choice
This or nothing.
Robin Hood's miles
Longer than usual.
Robin Hood's pennyworths

Rock
To be strong.
Rock
Certainty is a solid. (See: drifter, airhead).
Rocked in a stone cradle

Rod in pickle for you
A punishment awaiting one.
Rod of iron

Roll in dough
T
Roll out the red carpet
To treat royally.
Rollercoaster of emotions

of emotions, they are simply

downs.
Roman holiday

Rosetta Stone
*A
of something/one.*

Rough side downwards
Coarse-mannered, angry.

Rough-hewn
Plain, blunt, unpolished, ill-mannered

Roundabout is a turtle shell
A

Rug Rat
Infant

Rule out the possibility
T

denied.

Run away with
To do something impulsively.

Run like a skeiner
To move very fast.

Run out of gas
Lose impetus, begin to fail,

Run-of-the-mill
To be ordinary.

S

She's quite a catch
Meaning that a person is a good

Sacred cow
Ideal.

S

A

Safety-valve

Sail close to the wind
T
Salad bowl
A
retain their unique attributes.

Sandpaper

Say that one is about to explode
T
get very angry.

School is a gateway to adulthood
S
as an adult.

School ma'am(ish)

authority.

School your temper
B

Scrap-heap Pile of useless metal

Scratch the surface of...

on.

Scream the place down

Screw down on:...

Screw him up

a bargain or agreement.

Screw the nut
Pull yourself together.

Screwed up
Highly nervous.

Sea of grief
Very sad

Sealed off
Being impenetrable.

Sealed/closed book

Seamless web
Something without a pause.

Search-engine

words and phrases within a

Season of change

phases

Season
Current situation.
Seasoned

Secreted

Seduce
T

See red
To get angry.
See the color of someone's eyes
T

See what makes the wheels go round

Seeing pink elephants
H

Seize (up)

stress.
Send a baby on an errand
Invite failure by the way you

Send a husband into cornwall without a boat

Send a sow to minerva

oneself.
Send her down
Hughie! An appeal for rain or

Sermons in stones
Lessons learnt from nature.

Set a caird, and he'll ride to the devil
who have risen in the world.
Set high on the wheel
Be very fortunate.
Set him on his feet
Give him a new start.
Set the tortoise to catch the hare
Attempt the impossible.
Set the wheels in motion
T
Sets the low
Brings on herself the misfortune planned for another.
Seventh heaven
Highest level of bliss.
Shady character
A
Shake the lead out of your pants

Sharpen your pencil
T

She ran very fast/at a very high speed.
She followed in her mothers' footsteps
S
She had returned from the edge of death
She had almost died.
She is bewitching
S

She is his latest lover.
She is my better half
She is a better part of me.
Sheepish
To be embarrassed or shy.

Shift gears

to another, from one attitude, another.

Shift into top/high gear

Shining example of democracy
A

Shining example
T

Shock-absorber
Mitigating element in a potentially situation.

Shoed in the cradle and barefoot in the stubble
Prosperous in youth, poor in age.

Short-circuit

Short-circuit something
To do something, eliminating various intermediate steps..

Show one's true colours
T

Show someone the ropes
T

Shrew
A

Shrimp
Someone who is small.

Shunt into a siding
Relegate, postpone, treat with less

Shunt something somewhere else
Remove something that is unwanted or in the way.

Shut up like an oyster
T

Shuttle-witted
T

(A) Shylock
To be a heartless money-lender.

Side-slip
Deviate laterally from the previous

Side-track

evade the issue.

(A) Silver bullet
A straightforward solution that will have a sure and immediate

Singing the blues
Being sad.

Siren Dangerously

Sit on the safety-valve

Sketch in
Give a rough outline.

(To) Skid on...

-

(A) Skunk

Sky-pilot

Slack-spun
Retarded.

(A) Slate
S

Sleck-trough
Prostitute.

Sling ink

Sling mud
Defame, slander.
Slip the girths
Come to grief
Slippery slope
A small step may lead to a lot of

Sloth
To be very lazy.
Smell of the baby

Snail
A slow person.
Snake oil
F
Snake
T
Snowball effect
A
gradually builds up.
So mean he wouldn't give you a shock
If he owned the powerhouse
So unlucky

nose
(A) Soapbox
A

Soft sawder
Flattery.
Solder (up)
Repair.
Somewhere along the line

Son of the soil
Man who owes his living to the land.

Sound-barrier

preventing further progress.
Sour grapes!
Said of someone who, though badly wanting something, when he

Sow dragon's teeth
To invite enmity.
(A) Spanner

Span-new, spick and span
Fresh and smart.
Spare tyre
Roll of fat round the middle of a stout person.
Spark-plug

an inspiration.
Speak like an oracle

Speak volumes
T
Speaks as though he would creep into your mouth
Ingratiatingly.
Speck of dirt may clog the works of a watch
It needs very little to damage

Spell-bound
Captivated.
Spherical cow
S

Sphinx Enigmatic

S
A

S

Spin a long yarn
Exaggerate.
Spin a tale
Tell a story, usually a long exaggerated one.
Spin him/her to the length

S

Spin out
Be spent.
Spin out of control

allowed for.
Spin street-webs/street-yarn
Idle about the streets, gossiping
Spindle-shanks
Refers to someone having long, thin, tapering legs.
Spins his wheels

is ready for but prevented from

Spit for the white horse

Spit on his buttons

Spit on the same stone

Splinter group

Square one's loom
To punish someone.

Square peg in a round hole

Squeaking wheel never wears out
longest.
Stable
T
Stand on your own feet/legs
Be independent, self-reliant, manage without help.
S
mouths

Standing on the shoulders of giants
To develop further from what was established previously.
Star chamber
A
government that possesses the

government.
Star is in the ascendant
Rising in popularity.
Star is setting

Stare like
Bowse Beass Be inquisitive.
Steady rhythm
To be repeated over time is to be

Steam age...

fashioned
Steam ahead/along

Steamed up
So angry or passionate as to urge

Steam-roller
Crush opposition by weight rather

Steam-roller

authority slow, lumbering, insensitive, irresistible, levelling,

almost impossible to stop.
Steel your heart/yourself against/ to do something

yourself to/against...
Steer clear
To move away from.
Stench of failure

Step on the gas

Step up

Stooge

Stop ticking

Stop two mouths with one morsel

Story
B

Straight down the line
Without deviation, frills or

Strait the pin

Strand Recurring thread or streak in a character

Strange bedfellows
People who are generally not viewed together.

Strength and dignity are her clothing
Dignity matters more to her than fashion.
Stretch on the bed of Procrustes

something or someone.
Strike a chord

Strike a false note

Strike sparks out of...

Strike the right chord

response.
Strike the right note

Strike while the iron's hot

before it goes.
String together

(To be) Stubborn
To be persistent
Success is a sense of achievement, it is not an illegitimate child!

age-old belief that everyone wants

into an enterprise, the moment it

Such carpenters such chips

Suck dry

last penny.
Suck it all in
Understand as literal what was

Suck the blood of...

Suck the marrow out of life
To enjoy life to the fullest.
Sugar-tit

Sun over the yardarm
T

Swaddling clothes
Restraints on freedom.
Swallow the dictionary
Using long or unusual words.

Swan-song

Swear his ears through a two-inch board
Swear vehemently
Swear his ears through a two-inch board
Swear vehemently and against the

Sweat the lead out of...

situation.
Swept under the carpet
Hidden without resolving.
Swimming in a sea of diamonds
B
Swinging the lead
Avoid duty by feigning illness or injury.
Sword of Damocles
An ever-present threat.

T

Tail-spin chaos

Taj Mahal
L

Take a page out of someone's book(s)
To emulate somebody.

Take food out of the mouths of children
Cruelly to deprive the needy

Take someone to the cleaners
T

Take soundings
See how things are going.

Take the breeks off a Highlander

Take the ferry
To die.

Take the heat out of the situation

Take the rag off the bush
Surpass everything or everyone.

Take the rag off the hedge
Surpass, rouse admiration.

Take the rap

that has been done wrong by one.

Taken aback
T

Taken as
the whole meaning.

Tale in/of a tub

Tangle with
Confront.

Tank up

(To) Tantalize

(To) Tarnish (someone or something)
-

Teach your father to get children!

Teach someone a lesson

done wrong.

Tear someone apart
Ruthlessly destroy another

Tease out

Teddy bears' picnic

Teething troubles

something new.
Tell a tale

Tell tales out of school
T
damage.
Tell the tale

Tepid speech
A
That has been very hard to do
T
That is a horse of a very different color
That is a different matter altogether
That is cold comfort
R

but in reality, it is not
That is the way the cookie crumbles
T
That kindled love in his heart
S

That which will not be spun, let it not come between the spindle and the distaff

yourself in the way of it.
That's a different rub of the spindle
A different matter.
That's for the father and no for the son

it will not last a generation.
That's old Mother Hubbard!

Thats my mantra!
Belief or philosophy.
The anvil does not fear the hammer

The background

The best carpenters make the fewest chips!
Commenting that whores seldom

The best o' wabs are rough at the roons

at the beginning or end of their

The Big Apple
T
(USA).
The bitter end
Till the very end, be it rough or not.
The black bear of Arden

The blackest thoughts of men
T
The blues
Referring to sad songs.
The business was about to take

The business was about to start.
The carpenter is known by his chips

The clock is ticking
Time is running out
The close the book on something
A
The coast is clear
T

The cold wind of change
The unpleasant realities a new

The daddy of them all!

The damsel of the wood

The dog and his shadow

for the illusion.
The domino effect

The end of the bobbin
T
The end of the chapter
Till death.
The end of the rainbow

T
Our prize possession.
The farther from stone the better the church

expensive materials.
The father (and mother) of
Someone   or   something

T
yarn
One word or saying should not be
The golden ball rolls to everyone's feet once in a lifetime

in their life.
The hare and the tortoise

where the slow and steady one gains the ultimate advantage

opponent .

The height of one's career
H
The height of ten pennyworth of brass
Very small.
The honeymoon is over
R
are no longer enjoyable.
The light of my life

He or she is just someone who brings happiness or joy.
The little wimble will let in the great auger
Small beginnings lead to great

The loan of the oyster catcher to the seagull
The loan never repaid.
The man with the brass knackers
The boss.
The many-headed beast
Many of one thing.
The Midas touch

The milk of human kindness

The mountain was in labour and produceda mouse

The news made her very angry.
The noise is music to my ears
A
good news for the listener.
The nurse is valued till the child is done sucking

only while useful.

The nuts and bolts of...

of.
The one that got away
Somebody or something that

The pigeons fountained into the air
The great quantity of pigeons

off in groups to enlighten various people.
The point of conclusion
The end.
The raven said to the rook 'stand away, black coat!'

same.
The road to peace
A
The sea is a hungry dog
The sea swallows anything and

The shank of the evening/day
The last remaining part
The smith and his penny are both black

be inferred from the state of his property or relations.
The smith has always a spark in his throat
Thirsty.
The squeaky wheel gets the grease

response.
The steam that blows the whistle never turns the wheel

The swine has run through it
Of a marriage gone wrong.

The thread breaks where it is weakest
The failure of a person or enterprise originates from some

The tow

hopes.
The underdog
T
T

The waters of Lethe
oblivion.
The wheel has come full circle

The whiter the cow, the surer it is to go to the altar

The wish is father to the thought
We believe what we want to believe.
The witching hour

Theirs is a perfect match
T
There are fairies at the bottom of the garden

marvellous is happening hereabouts.
There were giants in those days
The men of old were better, mightier than modern men.
There's ay a wimple
S

fan it
Y
love in my heart.

They don't make 'em like that any more

day but now outmoded.
T
when he was young

They have more tow on their distaffs than they can well spin

They were "all over the place"

They were kindling a new romance
They were starting off with their

Thick as glue
T
something.
Thick as two Jews on a pay-day

Thick spinning
Bad behaviour, generally.
Thin as a witch's tit

Things are going smoothly
Things were going well.
Think/work along/on the same lines

but both using similar methods and moving towards the same

Thinks the sun shines out of his/her arse!

Third rail
A
pursuing it or even attempting to

This beats my grandmother
Of something astounding.
This won't buy the baby a new frock

Thread and thrum

Thread way
Through Pervade.
Throw a spanner in the works

Throw muck at...
Slander.
Throw of a loaded die
A
Throw on the scrap-heap

Throw out of gear/into neutral
Stop someone or something from

Throw the baby out with the bathwater
Be so intent on getting rid of what you do not want, that you also lose what you do want.
Thrum-head
Fool.
Thrummy-thrum

Thumb-nail sketch Brief

Tick over

Tiger
A positively aggressive person.
Tighter than a witch's cunt often of over

tops.
Tight-lipped
T

Till Los Angeles river wets its bed
Forever.
Till the cows comes home
For a very long time, perhaps, forever.
Tilt at windmills
T
Time is a thief

pass us by.
Time is money

Tin god
A
To a dot

To a shaving
P
To a tittle

To be poles apart
To have ideas that are very different
To be someone's Achilles' heel
T
otherwise strong position.
To cage
T

To disparage
To blame.
To drift apart
T

Tolerance is the window to peace
B
Tom prodger's job

Top dog
To be the best person.
Treat like dirt

Tried in the furnace
Severely tested.
Trip along

Triton among the minnows
A

those around him/her.
Trojan
A brave person.
(A) Troll
Stupid person.
Troy was not taken in a day
Used to signify to somebody to be patient.
Truth is Food

bitter for most palates, although the bitter foods are often the ones that nourish us most.
T
then in gold

liaisons of youth.

Tub-thumper
A
Tunnel vision
Condition of a diseased eye

and that a limited one.
Turkey
An idiot.
Turkeys voting for Christmas
A

Turn down a leaf
To stop for a while.
Turn over a new leaf
T
(A) Turntcoat
A
Turtle
Refers to a person who moves very slowly.
Twilight
Gloom.
Twine thread could have tied him!

U,V

Under her thumb

Under the aegis of...
to be under the leadership of.
Under the veneer of

Underline
To emphasise.
(To be) Unfold
Reveal
Unhewn
Rough, unpolished.
Unlicked cub
An ill-mannered youngster.
Unpolished

Unwind/wind down
Relax after a time of tension,

Up and down like a tinker's elbow
Often of something that has

(To be) Uptight
T
(A) Vegetable
Used to refer to a disabled or paralysed person.
Viper
Contemptible but dangerous and

Voice of a wolf
R
loud

Walk before you run/don't try to run before you can walk

Wander about like a lost soul
to roam around aimlessly and

Wander like a lost Jew
Roam about aimlessly.
Wants it like a baby wants its titty
With an urgent personal need, not so strongly felt by others.
Warm reception
A
Warp

Warts and all
With the unfavourable features as well as the favourable ones
Wash/wet the head of a new baby

Washing the Ethiop

Way-station

(have to) pass.

We are one
When two people are together they

We see not what sits on our shoulder

We were made for each other
W
other.
Weak sister

Wean from

Weasel out of
T
Weasel
A person who avoids.
Weathered
Aged.
Weave a tangled web

Weave a web of sorrow

uneasy or in trouble.
Weave about
T

(To) Weave
To build or plan or devise.
(To) Wed
T
Wedded to
T
something.
Wedge issue
A

(To) Weld
Join into a homogeneous unit

We'll just have to go our separate ways
W
other.
Well-oiled piece of machinery.

Well-oiled

Wet behind the ears

they are adult but should still, it

mothers.
Wet your whistle

(To) Whammy

What a story!
suggesting that what has been said

What makes them tick

Wheel within a wheel

or motives.

Wheels down! Prepare to leave
I warn you to leave very soon.
Wheels within wheels
C
Wheelstring job
Interminable.
When many strike on the anvil they must strike by measure
Where anything is in demand,

When the knot reaches the comb of the loom, you have to break the thread

When you're feelin' blue
When you are feeling low.

Where the rubber meets the road

membership.
Whip and a bell

Whipping boy

Whirlwind romance
R
brief
Whistle in the dark
T
one really has
Whistle-stop

inhabitants to warrant a
White as the driven snow
To be pure white.
White elephant
A very valuable but useless possession.

White glove
I
Whitestone days
To be remembered with pleasure.

wheel?
Putting in a great amount of effort for something trivial.
Why do you keep exposing your dull brain?

stupidity?
Win with a feather and lose with a straw
T
Wind him a pirn
T
Wind until a pirn
T
Wind up in...
End up in
Wind up
To end.
Wind up
T
Winds of change
R

Wired up

Wire-drawn
Of extreme or idle subtlety.
Wiry Lean
Sinewy and untiring.
Witch-hunt
A
enemies
With as good a will as ever I came from school
Gladly.

With open arms
T
Withers are unwrung
U
Wizard
Computer program enabling

Wolf in sheep's clothing
Evil person pretending to be friendly.
(A) Wolf
A negatively aggressive person.
Wooden-headed
Dull-witted. slow mentally.
Words are false idols
W
reality.
Work like a dog
H
Work overtime

Work the oracle
Obtain a favourable result by mysterious means.
Worth a Jew's eye
Very valuable.
Would charm the heart of a beggarman's crutch

Wouldn't give him the hole in a washer for it!

Wouldn't say boo to a battledore
Is very timid.

Wrangle for an ass's shadow

Wrapped
I
Wrapped around the axle

Wreathed in
Surrounded by.
Write the book
To be the main authority.
Written all over his face
Obvious.

Y, Z

Years know more than books
learning.
Yellow card
S
Yellow-bellied lizard
S
You are the light in my life
Y
happiness in my life.
You are the sun in my sky
T
that person the most important in

You can read his mind like an open book

You can't bore an auger hole with a gimlet

You can't drive a nail of wax

You can't judge a car by its paint job

You cry before you are hurt
Complain prematurely.
You had better pull your socks up
Get your life together.
You ride as if you went to fetch the midwife
To someone in great haste.
You're a pretty fellow to ride a goose a gallop through a dirty lane!

You're looking for maidenheads!

Your friendship is the picture to my frame
Having a memorable friendship

Your minnie's milk is not out of your nose yet
You are too young.
Zoom
Burst of energy, zest, drive.

SIMILES

Introduction

A Simile is a figure of speech that directly compares two things through some connective, usually "like," "as," "than," or a verb such as "resembles." A simile differs from a metaphor in that the latter compares two unlike things by saying that the one thing is the other thing.

Following is a list of Similes and their Meanings. Read, understand and learn them as they may be of great help in your day-to-day conversations and in making sentences as well as in writing good English.

A

As alike as two peas in a pod
I

As a bridegroom
Eager

As active as quicksilver
A

As afraid as a grasshopper
S

As ageless as the sun
Ageless

As agile as a cat
Agile

As agile as a monkey
Agile

As alert as a bird in springtime
Alert

As alike as two peas in a pod
I

As alert as chamois
Alert

As alone as a leper
Lonely

As alone as Crusoe
Alone

As ambitious as Lady Macbeth
Full of ambition

As American as apple pie
T

As ancient as the stars
Old

As ancient as the sun
Very old

As angry as a wasp
Anrgry

As arid as the sands of Sahara
Barren

A
F

A
A

As audacious as the day
Adventurous

As awful as justice
Awful

As awful as thunder
Very bad

As awkward as a cow on ice
V

B

As bad as a blight
Bad

As bad as the itch
Unbearable

As bald as a billiard ball
Bald

As bald as a coot
Bald

As bald as a coot
Bald

As bald as an egg
Bald

As bald as a coot
Completely bald

As bare as a lion
Bare

As bare as a stone
Bare

As barren as winter rain
Barren

As bashful as a schoolgirl
Shy

As beautiful as a rainbow
Very beautiful

As beautiful as the sunset
V

As big as a bus
Very big

As big as an elephant
Very big

As big as a whale
Very big

As big as an elephant
Huge

As big as the ocean
Huge

As bitter as death
Bitter, hard to absorb

As bitter as hemlock
Bitter

As bitter as wormwood
Very bitter

As black as a sweep
C

As black as coal
C

As black as pitch
C

As black as a crow
E

As black as a raven
P

As black as a sloe
V

As black as a starless night
B

As black as coal
B

As black as coal
V

As black as ebony
B
As black as ink
B
As black as jet
B
As black as Newgate's knocker
B
As black as sin
V
As black as soot
B
As black as the ace of spades
B
As black as the earl of hell's waistcoat
B
As black as thunder
B
As black as your hat
B
As blameless as the snow
I
As blank as an empty bottle
C
As blind as a bat
Blind
As blind as a bat
Not able to see
As blind as a bat
Blind, unable to see
As blind as a bat
Completely blind
As blind as a beetle
C
As blind as a mole
Blind
As blind as a mole
B
As blind as ignorance
Blind

A
Carefree
As blithe as May
Carefree
As blue as forget me not
Blue
As blue as indigo
P
As blunt as a hammer
Blunt
As blut as the back of a knife
Blunt
As blind as a bat
Completely blind
As blind as a mole
Completely blind
As bold as brass
Very bold
As boisterous as stormy sea winds
V
As bold as a lion
Sassy
As boring as a wet weekend in Wigan
Boring
As boring as watching paint dry
Boring
As boundless as the ocean
Limitless
As bounteous as nature
R
As brainless as a chimpanzee
Dumb
As brave as a lion
Very brave
As brave as a soldier
Very gutsy
As brave as Achilles
Brave
As brief as a dream
Small time

As bright as a button
Very bright
As bright as a new pin
Very bright and shiny
As brief as time
Of small duration
As bright as a button
Bright
As bright as a lark
Bright
As bright as a new penny
Bright
As bright as a new pin
Bright
As bright as a new shilling
Shiny
As bright as day
Very bright
As bright as noon day
Very bright and shiny
As bright as silver
Very bright
As bright as the light
Bright
As bright as the sun
Bright
As brilliant as a mirror
Brilliant
As brilliant as the stars
Brilliant
As brisk as a bailiff
Alert
A
Adroit
A
Agile
As brittle as glass
Fragile

As broad as heaven's expanse
Broad
As broad as it is long
Broad
As brown as a berry
Brown
As brown as a bun
Brown
As brown as hazelnuts
Brown
As brown as Mahogany
B
As buoyant as wings
V
As busy as a beaver
Very busy
As busy as a bee
Very busy
As busy as a cat on a hot tin roof
Very busy
As busy as a bee
Busy
As busy as a bee
Very busy
As busy as a cat on a hot tin roof
Very busy
As busy as a nailer
H
As busy as a one-armed paper hanger
O
As busy as a one-legged arse kicker
P
As busy as an ant
B

C

As calm as a cat
C

As calm as a millpond
V

As calm as a summer sea
V

As calm as death
Calm

As calm as glass
Calm

As careless as the wind
Carefree

As cautious as a fox
W

As cautious as a Scot
Alert

As camp as a row of tents
Camp

As candid as mirrors
V

As clean as a whistle
V

As clear as crystal
V

As clear as mud
N

As cold as ice
V

As common as dirt
V

As certain as Christmas
Sure

As certain as the rising of the morning sun
Sure to happen

As changeable as the moon
Variable

As changeable as the weather
Variable

As chaste as a lily
Pure

As chaste as Minerva
Chaste

As cheap as dirt
Cheap

As cheap as lies
Cheap

As cheeky as a young bantam cock
C

As cheerful as a lark
Happy

As cheerful as the birds
Cheerful

As cheerful as the day is long
Happy

As cheerless as the grave
Sad

As cheery as a sunbeam
Cheerful

As chill as death
Cold
As chilly as a tomb
Chilly
As chubby as a cherub
Chubby
As clammy as death
Clammy
As clean as a Dutch oven
Neat
As clean as a hound's tooth
V
As clean as a new pin
Tidy
As clean as a whistle
Clean
As clear as a bell
Clear
As clear as crystal
Clean, transparent
As clear as day
Clear
As clear as daylight
Flawless
As clear as mud

As clear as noonday
Unblemished
As clear as rock water
Pure
As clear as said of tones
Clear
As clever as paint
Clever
As clumsy as a bear
Clumsy
As coarse as fustian
Rough
As coarse as hemp
Stiff

As cold as a corpse
Cold
As cold as a dog's nose
Cold

(unemotional)
As cold as a frog
Cold
As cold as a stone
Cold, emotionless
As cold as a well digger's arse
Cold
As cold as a witch's tit
Cold
As cold as any stone
Cold/Emotionless
As cold as blue blazes
Cold
As cold as charity
Emotionless
As cold as ice
V
As cold as marble
Cold
As common as dirt
E
As common as muck
Common
As common as pins
Common
As common as poverty
Common
As complacent as a cat
S
A
Self-assured
A
C
As conscientious as a dog
Careful

As consoling as night
Soothing

As contagious as a yawn
I

As contrary as black and white
Contrasting

As contrary as light and darkness
Contrary

As convincing as the multiplication table
Persuasive

As cool as a cucumber
C

As costly as an election
Expensive

As countless as hairs
Limitless

As countless as the desert sands
Countless

As countless as the stars
U

As cowardly as a wild duck
S

As cozy as the nest of a bird
Comfortable

As crafty as a fox
C

As crazy as a loon
L

As credulous as a child
Credulous

As crisp as new bank notes
Crisp

As crooked as a corkscrew
Bent

As crooked as a dog's hind leg
C

As cross as two sticks
Cross

As cruel as Media
U

As cruel as winter
Cruel

As cunning as a fox
Sly

As cunning as a monkey
Crafty

A
Keen

As cute as a baby
V

As cute as a bug's ear
Adorable

As cute as a button
Cute, adorable

As cute as a button
Cute

As cute as a cup cake
Cute

D

As daft as a brush
Daft
As damp as the salty blue ocean
Wet
As dangerous as machine guns
Threatening
As dark as a dungeon
D
As dark as midnight
D
As dark as pitch
D
As dead as a doornail
Dead
As dead as the dodo
D
As dead as a dodo
E
As dead as a door nail
Dead
As dead as a doornail
Dead beyonad doubt
As dead as a herring
D
As dead as mutton
Lifeless
As dead as the Roman Empire
With no life
As dead as wood
Dead

As deaf as a beetle
Deaf
As deaf as a post
Completely deaf
As deaf as the billows
C
As deceitful as the devil
D
As deceptive as the mirage of the desert
D
As deep as a draw well
Very deep
As deep as a well
Deep
As deep as despair
Of great depth
As deep as hell
Unfathomable
As deep as the sea
Very deep
As dejected as a wet hen
Gloomy

Fragile
As delicious as a dream
Desirable
As delicious as forbidden fruit
Tempting
As dense as a brick
Very dense

As desolate as a tomb
Isolated
As devoted as a faithful dog
S
As devoted as a mother
Devoted
As different as chalk from cheese
Very different
As different as chalk from cheese
Opposite
A
Tough
A
D

Hard
As dirty as a hog
Dirty
As dirty as a pig
Dirty
As disappointing as wet gunpowder
Disappointing
As dismal as a hearse
Sad
As distant as the horizon
Far
As dizzy as a goose
Dizzy
As docile as a lamb
I
As dreadful as a gathering storm
Dangerous
As dreary as an Asian steppe
Boring
As dreary as an empty house
Dull
T

As drunk as a beggar
D

A
D
A
Out of his senses
As drunk as a lord
E
As drunk as a skunk
D
As drunk as a top
D

V
As drunk as a lord
C
As dry as a biscuit
Dry
As dry as a bone
Extremely dry
As dry as a bone
Dry
As dry as a mummy
Dry
As dry as a pommy's bath towel
Dry
As dry as a stick
Dry
As dry as dust
Dry
As dull as dishwater
Very dull
As dull as ditch water
Unpleasant
As dull as lead
Dull
As dumb as a box of rocks
Dumb
As dumb as a mouse
Stupid
As dumb as a statue
Dumb
As dumb as any oyster
Dumb
As dumb as stone
Dumb

E

As easy as apple-pie
Very easy

To eat like a bird
To eat very little

To eat like a horse
To eat a lot

As easy as ABC
Simple

As easy as falling off a log
Easy

As easy as lying
Simple

As easy as pie
Very easy

As easy as shelling peas
Simple

As easy as taking candy from a baby
Simple

As easy as winking
Simple

As elastic as a caterpillar
Flexible

As eloquent as Cicero
Fluent

As elusive as quicksilver
Elusive

As empty as an idiot's mind
B

As empty as space
Empty

As enticing as a riddle
A

As essential as the dew
Needed

As expensive as glory
P

F

As fabulous as Aladdin's ring
Amazing
As faint as the hum of distant bees
Faint
As fair as a rose
Fair
As fair as Eve in paradise
Flawless
As fair as the morn
Fair
As fair as truth
Right
As faithful as the dog
Faithful
As faithful as the sun
Dependable
As faithless as fair weather
Faithless
As false as dice
Untrue
As familiar as a popular song
Known by heart
As familiar as an oath
Known
As far apart as the poles
Opposites
As far as the eye can see
Distant

As far as the poles asunder
Distant
As fast as a deer
Q
As fast as a hare
Rapid
As fast as a horse
Very fast, speedy
As fast as a racecar
Very fast, speedy
As fast as a storm
Q
As fast as an eagle
Q
As fast as greased lightening
Speedy
As fast as light
Q
As fat as a distillery pig
Fat
As fat as a hippo
Very fat
As fat as a pig
Fat
As fat as a porpoise
Fat
As fat as a quail
Fat

As fat as a sheep's tail
  Weighty
As fat as a whale
  Fat
As fat as butter
  Fat
As feeble as a child
  W
A
  Changing
A
  F
A
  F
A
  Fidgety
A
  Angry
A
  F
A
  F
A
  Stern

  Fine
A
  Firm
A
  Rigid
A
  Firm
A
  Firm
A
  Firm

  Very healthy

  Fit

Fit
A
  U
A
and the Persians
  Fixed
A
  Flabby
A
  Flat
A
  C
A
  Flat
A
  Flat
A
  Flat
A
  Thin
A
  Fragile
As foolish as a calf
  Silly
As foul as a sty
  Unpleasant
As foul as slander
  Foul
As frail as a lily
  I
A
  Fragile
As frail as glass
  W
As free as a bird
  Free
As free as a breeze
  Free
As free as a daisy
  Free

A
Free
As free as the air
Free
As free as thought
Free
As fresh as a daisy
Fresh
As fresh as a mountain stream
Fresh
As fresh as dew
Fresh
As fresh as paint
Fresh
As fresh as a daisy
Very fresh
As fresh as rose
Fresh
As fresh as sea breeze
Fresh
As friendless as an alarm clock
Lonely
As friendly as a puppy
Playful
As frightened as Macbeth before the ghost of Banquo
S

As frigid as an iceberg
Frigid
As frisky as a kitten
F
As frisky as a lamb
E
As frisky as a two year old
E
As frisky as colts
F
As frizzled as a lawyer's wig
Frizzled
As fruitful as Egypt
Useful
As full as a fat lady's sock
Full
As full as an Alabama tick
Full
As full as an egg is of meat
Done
As funny as a balloon
V
As funny as a circus
Amusing

G

A
In good spirits
As garrulous as a magpie
T
As garrulous as an old maid
Chatty
A
Gaudy
As gaudy as a peacock
Gaudy
A
Happy
As gay as a lark
Happy
As gay as the spring
Happy
As generous as a dream
Generous
As generous as a lord
Generous
As genial as sunshine
Genial
As gentle as a dove
Gentle
As gentle as a fawn
Gentle
As gentle as a lamb
I
As gentle as falling dew

Calm, tender
As gentle as sleep
Gentle
As gentle as turtle dove
Tender
As glad as a blooming tree
Happu
A
Happy
As glib as glass
Glib
As gloomy as night
Gloomy
As glorious as the sun
Glorious
As glossy as a mole
Glossy
A
Shiny
As glum as an oyster
Glum
As glum as mud
Glum
As gluttonous as curiosity
Gluttonous
As good as a play
G
As good as it gets
Very good

As good as new
Good
As good as your word
Great
As good as gold
Very good and obedient
As gorgeous as a Sultan
Gorgeous
As gorgeous as the heavens
Marvellous
As graceful as a fawn
G
As graceful as a swan
G
As gracious as a duchess
Giving
As gracious as the morn
G
As grand as a Greek statue
Grand
As grand as a victory
V
As grand as the world
Vast
As grasping as a miser
Grasping

As grave as a judge
Grave
As great as a lord
Great, powerful
As greedy as a cormorant
Greedy
As greedy as a dog
Greedy
As greedy as a hog
Greedy
As greedy as a pig
Greedy
As greedy as a wolf
Greedy
As grey as smoke
Shady
As grey as time
Grey
As grim as death
Sad
As grim as hell
Grim
As gruff as a bear
Gruff

H

As haggard as specters
Fatigues
As hairless as an egg
Hairless
As hairy as a gorilla
Hairy
As hairy as a mastodon
Hairy
As hairy as a spider
Hairy
As hairy as an ape
Very hairy
As handsome as paint
Handsome
As happy as a child
Happy
As happy as a clown
Happy
As happy as a dog with two tails
Happy
As happy as a king
Happy
As happy as a lord
Glad
As happy as a lark
Very happy
As happy as a pig in shit
Merry
As happy as a rat with a gold tooth
Very happy

As happy as a sandboy
Happy
As happy as Larry
Very happy
As happy as the day is long
Happy
As hard as a rock
Hard
As hard as a stone
H
A
Hard
As hard as nails
V
As hard as granite
Hard
As hard as horn
Hard
As hard as iron
Hard
As hard as marble
Solid

As hard as nails
H
As hard as steel
Hard
As harmless as a babe
Harmless
As harmless as a dove
Of no danger
As harsh as a grating wheel
Harsh
As harsh as truth
Tough
A
Q
As hateful as death
Hateful
As haughty as a devil
Arrogant
As healthy as a May morning
Good
As hearty as an oak
Hearty
As heavy as a bag of sand
Heavy
As heavy as an elephant
Heavy
As heavy as lead
Heavy
As heavy as sand
Weighty
As helpless as a babe
Helpless
As helpless as a baby
Helpless
As hideous as the witch of Endor
Ugly
As high as a kite
Very high
As high as heaven
Distant

As high as the stars
High
As hoarse as a crow
H
As hollow as a drum
Hollow
As honest as a mirror
Truthful
As honest as the day is long
Honest
As hopeful as the break of day
Full of hope
As horny as a camel's knee
Horny
As horrid as a murderer's dream
Horrid

Extremely hot
As hot as a furnace
Hot
As hot as hell
Very hot
As hot as an over
Very hot
As hot as blue blazes
Hot
A
Hot
As hot as molten lead
Hot
As hot as pepper
Hot
As hueless as a ghost
Colorless
As huge as high Olympus
Great
As humble as a worm
Humble
As humble as Uriah Heep
Kind

As humorous as wind
  Humorous
As hungry as a bear
  Starving
As hungry as a church's mouse
  Starving
As hungry as a bear
  Very hungry
As hungry as a wolf
  Very hungry
As hungry as a hawk
  Hungry

As hungry as a horse
  Hungry
As hungry as a hunter
  Hungry
As hungry as a wolf
  Famished
As hungry as the grave
  Hungry
As hushed as midnight.
  Silent

I

As idle as a Lazzarone
Lazy
As idle as air
Indolent
As ignorant as a child
Ignorant
As illimitable as the boundless sea
Limitless
As illusive as a dream
Illusive, not real
As imitative as a monkey
Uninspired
As immaculate as an angel
P
As immense as the sea
Bountiful
As immortal as the stars
Eternal
As immutable as the laws of the Medes and the Persians
Absolute
As impatient as a lover
Impatient
As imperishable as eternity
Eternal
As impetuous as a poet
Impetuous

As innocent as a lamb
I
As inconstant as the moon
V
As inconstant as the waves
Variable
As indolent as an old bachelor
Indolent
As industrious as a beaver
Organized
As inevitable as death
Unavoidable
As inexhaustible as the deep sea
Inexhaustible
As inexorable as a grave
Inexorable
A
N
As innocent as a dove
I
As innocent as a lamb
I
As invisible as the air
Not there
As Irish as Paddy's pig
Irish

J,K

As jealous as a cat
Envious

As jealous as a Spaniard
Jealous

As jolly as a sandboy
Jolly

As jolly as a shoe brush
Happy

A
Fun

As joyous as the laughter of a child
Joyous

As jubilant as old sleigh bells
Jubilant

As keen as a razor
Curious

As keen as hunger
Curious

As keen as mustard
K

As killing as a plague
Killing

As kind as consent
Kind

As kind as jesus
V

As knowing as the stars
Knowledgeable

L

As languid as a love-sick maid
L
As large as life
H
As lasting as the pyramids
Ever lasting
As lavish as the moon
Extravagant
As lawful as eating
Legal
As lawless as the stormy wind
Senseless
As lax as cut string
Lax
As lazy as a lobster
Lazy
As lazy as a pig
Lazy
As lazy as a ship in the doldrums
Lazy
As lazy as a toad
Lazy
As lean as a lath
Thin
As lean as a skeleton
Lean
As lean as Sancho's ass
Slender

To leak like a sieve
Full of holes
As lenient as soft opiates to the mind
Linient
As level as a pond
B
As liberal as the sun
Independent
As lifeless as the grave
Lifeless
As light as a feather
Weightless
As light as air
Very light
As light as a cork
Light
As light as a feather
Weightless
As light as air
Weightless, lightweight
As light as down
Light
As light as thistle down
Light
As like as two beans
I
As like as two drops of water
I

As like as two herring
Same
As like as two peas
Same
Like a cat on a hot tin roof
Jumpy, nervous
Like the wind

Like two clappers
Very rapidly
Like a newly hatched chick
Brand new, fresh
Like a soldier on a mission
F
Like a ton of bricks
Very heavy
As lithe as a panther
Agile
As lithe as a tiger
Supple
As little as a squirrel
Tiny
As little as Tom Thumb
Little
As lively as a cricket
Cheerful
As loathsome as a toad
Hateful
As lonely as a deserted ship
Lonely
As lonely as the Arctic Sea
Alone

As long as a month of Sundays
Lengthy
As long as my arm
Long
As loose as a goose
Loose
As loose as a rope of sand

As loquacious as Polonius
T
As loud as a horn
Loud
As loud as a lion
Loud
As loud as thunder
I
As lovely as love
Very lovely
As lovely as the violet
Lovely
As lovely as Venus
Lovely
As low as the grave
Low
As lowly as a slave
Lowly
As lowly as a worm
Low
As loyal as an apostle
Loyal

M

As mad as a bear with a sore head
Mad
As mad as a hornet
Mad
As mad as a March hare
Crazy
As mad as a wet hen
Very mad
As mad as a hatter
C
As mad as a hornet
Very angry
As mad as the march hare
V
As magnanimous as Agamemnon
Magnanimous
As malicious as Satan
M
As many chins as a Chinese phone book
Abundant
As mean as a miser
Mean
As meek as a dove
M
As meek as a lamb
M
As meek as a mouse
M

Memory like a sieve
To have a poor memory, to have

As merciless as ambition
T
As merciless as Othello
M
As merciless as the grave
Unsparing
As merry as a cricket
Happy
As merry as a lark
Glad
As merry as spring
Happy
As mighty as a king
Mighty
As mild as a dove
Mild
As mild as milk
B
As mild as moonlight
Mild
Mind like a sieve
To have a poor memory, to have

As mischievous as a kitten
Naughty, troublesome
As mischievous as a monkey
Naughty

As miserable as sin
  Miserable
As mobile as humanity
  Mobile
As modest as a dove
  Modest
As modest as a maiden
  Modest
As modest as a primrose
  Humble
As monotonous as the sea
  Routine
As motionless as a corpse
  Still
As mournful as the grave
  Sad
As much use as a yard of pump water
  A lot

As muddy as sheep dogs
  Dirty
As mum as an oyster
  Shut
A
  Silent
As mute as mice
  Silent, mute
As mute as the grave
  Mute
As mute as the tomb
  Q
As mysterious as a sphinx
  M
As mysterious as an echo
  Mysterious
As mysterious as dove
  Mysterious

N

As naked as a baby
N
As naked as a jaybird
Exposed
As naked as a peeled apple
N
As naked as night
N
As natural as life
Natural
As near as dammit
Close
As nearsighted as a mole
Short sighted
As neat as a nail
Neat
As neat as a new pin
Tidy
As neat as ninepins
Neat
As needful as the sun
Needful
As nervous as a long tailed cat in a room full of rocking chairs
Very anxious
As nervous as a mouse
Nervous

As nervous as a whore in church
Nervous
As new as day
New, Fresh
As nice as ninepence
Pleasant
As nimble as a bee
Agile
As nimble as a squirrel
Nimble
As nimble as lizard
Alert
As nimble as quicksilver
Agile
As noiseless as a shadow
Silent
As noisy as a menagerie
Noisy
As numerous as the sands upon the ocean shore
Numerous
As nutty as a fruitcake
C

O

As obedient as a puppet
Obedient

As obedient as the scabbard
Dutiful

As obnoxious as an alligator
Irritating

As obstinate as a mule
Very obstinate, stubborn

As obstinate as a mule
Stubborn

As obstinate as a pig
Obstinate

As old as creation
A

As old as dirt
Very old

As old as methuselah
A

As old as the hills
A

As opaque as the sky
Opaque

As open as a smile
Open

As open as day
Open

As opposite as the poles
Opposite

Out like a light

P

As pale as death
V

As pale as death
Extremely pale

As pale as a ghost
Pale

As passionate as young love
P

As patient as an ox
Patient

As patient as the hours
Patient

As peaceful as sleep
Harmonious

As persistent as a mosquito
Determined

As piercing as light
P

As pissed as a newt
Pissed

As pissed as a rat
Pissed

As placid as a duck pond
P

As plain as a pikestaff
Plain, simple

As plain as day
Plain, nothing interesting

As plain as the nose on your face
Flat

As plain as day
V

A
Friendly

As playful as a kitten
Playful

As playful as a puppy
Friendly

As playful as a rabbit
Funny and playful

As playful as a squirrel
Playful

As pleasant as health
Pleasant

As pleased as punch
Very pleased

As plentiful as ants
Abundant

As plentiful as blackberries
Ample

As plump as mastiffs
Plump

As plump as partridge
Plump

As polite as wax
Polite

As poor as a church mouse
P

As poor as dirt
Poor

As poor as lazarus
P
As populous as an ant hill
Populous
As positive as a scotsman
O
As powerful as a lion
Strong
As powerful as death
Powerful
As powerless as an infant
Helpless
As pretty as a picture
V
As pretty as paint
Pretty
As progressive as time
A
As proud as a peacock
Extremely proud, arrogant
As proud as Lucifer
Proud

As proud as Punch
Arrogantly proud
As punctilious as a Spaniard
Assiduous
As punctual as a springtime
On time
As pure as snow
P
As pure as the driven snow
P
As pure as a lily
True, spotless
As pure as faith
True
As pure as snow
Pure, virgin
As pure as winter snow
Pure
As purple as the heather
Purple

Q

As quarrelsome as the weasel
Troublesome

As queer as a chocolate orange
Strange

As queer as a nine bob note
Weird

As queer as folk
Queer

A
Q

As quick as a lamplighter
Sudden

As quick as a lightning
I

As quick as a weasel
Speedy

As quick as thought
Rapid

As quick as a wink
V

As quick as lightning
V

As quick as silver
V

As quiet as a church mouse
Very quiet

As quiet as a lamb
Noiseless

As quiet as a mouse
Silent

R

As ragged as Lazarus
Ragged

As rapid as lightning
Sudden

As rare as a blue rose
Rare

As rare as a comet
H

As rare as hens' teeth
S

As rare as rocking horse shit
Rare

As ravenous as a winter wolf
Ravenous

As real as the stars
Real, true

As rebellious as the sea
R

As red as a beetroot
Red

As red as a cherry
Red

As red as a clown's nose
Very red

As red as a poppy
Red

As red as a rose
Red

As red as a turkey-cock
Red

As red as blood
Red

As red as crimson
Red

A
R

As red as scarlet
Red

Red as a beet
Embarrassed

As regal as Juno
Regal

As regular as clockwork
Mundane

As regular as sunrise
Regular

As regular as the clock
Regular

As relentless as fate
Relentless

As remote as a dream
Remote

As resistless as the wind
Resistless

As restless as ambition
Restless

As restless as the sea
Impatient

As rich as a Jew
R

As rich as careole
Very wealthy
As rich as Croesus
R
As rich as gold
R
As right as nails
Right
As right as ninepence
Feel well
As right as rain
To feel well
As ripe as a cherry
Ripe, developed
As rosy as a bride
Blushing
As rotten as dirt
Rotten
As rough as a storm
Rough
As rough as hemp
Rough

As round as a ball
Round
As round as a barrel
C
As round as a globe
Round
As round as a sphere
Round
As round as an apple
Round
As round as an orange
Round
As round as the O of Giotto
Round
As rude as a bear
Rude
As rugged as a rhinoceros
Rugged
Run like the wind
R
As ruthless as the sea
Ruthless

S

As sacred as a shrine
S
As sad as doom
M
As sad as night
Sad
As safe as houses
V
As safe as a sardine
Safe
As safe as a tortoise under its shell
S
As safe as blackhouse
S
As safe as houses
Very safe, haven
As safe as the Bank of England
S
As safe as the bank
Safe
As salt as a herring
Salt
As salt as sea sponge
Salty
As salty as brine
Salty
As saucy as the wave
S
A
Rare

As secret as thought
S
As secure as the grave
Safe
As scarce as hen's teeth
V
As seedy as a raspberry
Seedy
A
S
As senseless as stones
I

D
As serious as a doctor
Serious
As serious as an owl
Serious
As shallow as a pan
Shallow
As shameless as a nude statue
Shameless
As shameless as sin
I
As shapeless as an old shoe
Shapeless
As sharp as a razor
Very sharp
As sharp as a lance
Sharp, edgy
As sharp as a needle
Sharp

As sharp as a tack
Sharp
As sharp as a thistle
Sharp
As shiny as a new pin
Shiny
As short as any dream
Short
As short as the life of a wave
Small lived
As shy as a schoolgirl
Shy
As shy as the fawn
Introvert
As shy as the squirrel
Introvert
As sick as a dog
V
As sick as a parrot
V
As sick as a dog
Ill
As sick as a parrot
Ill
As silent as the dead
Completely silent
As silent as the grave
Completely silent
As silent as a stone
Noiseless
As silent as the dead
Extremely silent
As silent as the grave
Mute
As silent as the stars
Quiet
As silent as thought
Noiseless
As silly as a goat
Absurd

As silly as a goose
Very foolish, silly
As silly as a sheep
Silly
As silly as calves
Absurd
As simple as A B C
Easy
As simple as a child
Simple
As sincere as sunlight
S
As skinny as a rake
Slim
Sleep like a baby
Sleeping soundly
As sleek as a mouse
S
To sleep like a log
To sleep soundly.
As sleepless as owls
Sleepless
As sleepy as a koala
Sleepy
As slender as a thread
Slender
As slender as gossamer
Slender
As slippery as an eel
Slippery, evasive, not to be trusted

(a person who is not trustworthy)
As slippery as a serpent
Untrusted
As slippery as ice
Slippery
As slow as a snail
With no speed
As slow as a turtle
S
As slow as a wet weekend
Slow

As slow as molasses
Moves very slowly
As slow as molasses in January
Slow
As slow as molasses
Slow
As sly as a fox
Cunning
As sly as a fox
S
As small as a sixpence
Small, tiny
As small as atoms
Tiny
As small as paint
Small
As small as the hairs on a gnat's bollock
Small
As smart as albert einstein
Intelligent
As smart as an owl
Smart
To smoke like a chimney

As smooth as silk
Very smooth
As smooth as a baby's bottom
Smooth
As smooth as butter
Smooth
As smooth as glass
Smooth
As smooth as glass
F
As smooth as ice
Smooth
As smooth as oil
Smooth
As smooth as silk
S
As smooth as velvet
F

As snug as a bug in a rug
Comfortable
As sober as a judge
Sober, sane
As soft as a baby's bottom
Soft
As soft as butter
Soft
As soft as down
Soft
As soft as fur
Soft
As soft as putty
Gentle
As soft as silk
Very soft
As soft as velvet
Soft
As soft as wax
Soft
As soft as wool
Soft
As solid as the ground we stand on
Solid
As solid as a rock
Solid, hard
As solid as bricks
Solid
As solitary as a tomb
Solitary
As soothing as the breath of spring
Soothing
As sound as a bell
Sane
As sour as vinegar
Very sour
As sour as crab
Sour
As sour as lime
Sour
As spacious as the element
S

As speechless as a stone
Quiet
A
Spineless
As spiteful as a monkey
Spiteful
As spotless as lilies
Flawless
As spotless as snow
Spotless
As stale as old beer
Stale, old
As stately as an oak
Stately
As steadfast as a queen
Steadfast
As steady as a rock
Steady
As steady as the sun
Steady
As stealthy as a cat
S
As stealthy as a rock
S
As stern as a judge
Stern
As sticky as jam
S
As stiff as a board
Completely stiff
As stiff as a board
Stiff, hard to bend
As stiff as a poker
Stiff not giving anything away
As stiff as a ramrod
Rigid
As stiff as a stone
Stiff
As stiff as death
Stiff
As still as a log
Still

As still as a post
Unmoving
As still as a statue
Unmoving
As still as death
Not moving
As still as the grave
Unmoving
As stink as a polecat
S
As stinky as carrion
S
As stolid as a cow
Impassive
As straight as an arrow
Straight
As straight as a candle
Straight
As straight as a die
Straight
As straight as an arrow
Straight
As strange as a vision
Queer
Strong as an ox
Very strong
As strong as a horse
Strong
As strong as a lion
M
As strong as brandy
Resilient
As strong as hercules
Strong
As stubborn as a mule
Obstinate
As stubborn as a mule
Stubborn
As stupid as a donkey
Stupid
As stupid as a log
Stupid
As stupid as a post
I

As stupid as a sloth
Supid

As stupid as an ass
I

As stupid as an oak
Stupid

Sturdy as an oak tree
Very strong

As subtle as a serpent
Subtle

As sudden as a snap
S

As sudden as lightning
Rapid

As sulky as a bear
S

A
S

As superstitious as sailors
Irrational

As supple as a snake
Agile

As sure as a gun
Sure

As sure as death
Certain, unavoidable

As sure as death and taxes
A

As sure as eggs is eggs
V

As sure as fate
U

As sure as God made little green apples
Certain

As sure as sunrise
Certain

As sure-footed as a goat
S

As surly as a bear
Gruff

As suspicious as a cat
S

As sweet as a nut
Sweet

As sweet as a rose
Sweet

As sweet as honey
Sweet

As sweet as pie
Sweet

As sweet as sugar
Very sweet

As swift as a deer
Q

A
Sudden

As swift as a hare
Sudden

As swift as a hawk
Sudden

As swift as an arrow
Rapid

As swift as an eagle
Q

As swift as lightning
Swift

As swift as the wind
Swift

As swift as thought
Swift

T

As talkative as a magpie
T

Tall as a tree
Very tall

As tall as a giant
Tall

As tall as a giraffe
Very tall

As tall as a poplar
Tall

As tall as a steeple (mast)
Very tall

As tall as maypole
Very tall

As tame as a chicken
Tame

As tame as a hare
Tame

As tame as a house cat
Tame

As tame as a sheep
Tame

A
Taut

As tedious as a guilty conscience
Mind-numbling

As tenacious as a bull-dog
Stubborn

As tender as a bud
Gentle

As tender as chicken
Soft

As tender as lamb
Tender

As tender as shepherd
Soft

As tender as tears
Gentl

As terrible as hell
Horrible

Thick as a brick
Not very smart

As thick as a brick
T

As thick as a cable
T

As thick as ants
T

As thick as blackberries
T

As thick as hail
T

As thick as thieves
T

As thick as thieves
Close friends

As thick as two short planks
T

As thin as a lath
Thin

As thin as a rail
Thin
As thin as a rake
Thin
As thin as a wafer
Thin
As thirsty as a sponge
Thirsty
As thirsty as tantalus
Thirsty
As thoughtless as a lark
Thoughtless
As tidy as a candy shop
Clean
As tight as a drum head
Tight
As tight as a drum
Tight
As tight as a duck's arse
Tight
As tight as Dick's hatband
Tight
As tight as teeth
Tight
As tight as wax
Tight
As timid as a rabbit
Very timid
As timid as a fawn
Timid
As timid as a mouse
Timid
As timid as a rabbit (as a hare)
Timid
As timid as a rabbit
Timid
As tiny as a grain of sand
Small
As tired as a runner after marathon
Exhausted
As tired as tombstones
Exhausted

As tough as leather
Very tough
As tough as nails
Very tough
As tough as old boots
Very tough
As tough as leather

As tough as leather
Tough
As tough as nails
Very tough, hard
As tough as old boots
D
As trackless as the desert
T
As trackless as the sea
T
As tranquil as the summer sea
P
As transient as lightning
Transient
As transparent as glass
See through
As treacherous as the memory
Unfaithful
As tricky as a box of monkeys
T
As tricky as an ape (a monkey)
T
As trivial as a parrot's prate
I
As troublesome as a monkey
Naughty
As true as steel
True
As true as the gospel
True
As truthful as a knight of old
Truthful
As tuneless as a bag of wool
Tuneless

U

As ugly as a bear
Ugly
As ugly as a scarecrow
Ugly
As ugly as a toad
Ugly
As ugly as an ape
Ugly
As ugly as sin
Ugly
As unapproachable as a star
Distant
As unattractive as a gargoyle
Not beautiful
As uncertain as the weather
U
As unchangeable as the past
Fixed
As unclean as sin
Impure
As uncomplaining as a lamb
A
As uncompromising as justice
Rigid
As unconquerable as chewing gum
I
As uncontrollable as the wave
O
As unfeeling as rocks
Cold

As unhappy as King Lear
Sad
As universal as light
Universal
As universal as seasickness
Universal
As unmerciful as the billows
T
A
U
As unreal as a dream
Not true
As unstable as the wind
Unstable
As unstable as water
Unstable
As unsteady as the ocean
Unsteady
As unusual as a sailor on horseback
Strange
As upright as a tower
Straight and tall
As useful as a cow
P

Useless
As useless as a chocolate teapot
Useless

V

As vague as a shadow
N

As vague as futurity
Vague

As vain as a peacock
Futile

As various as the weather
E

As vast as eternity
Boundless

As venomous as a snake
Poisonous

As vigilant as the stars
A

As
Vigorous

As violent as steam
Violent, noisy

As virtuous as holy truth
Holy

As voiceless as the tomb
Spineless

As vulgar as money
I

W

As warm as toast
Warm

As weak as a kitten
W

As weak as gnat's piss
W

As welcome as a skunk at a lawn party
N

As well as can be expected
Very well

As white as a ghost
V

As white as a sheet
Pure white

As white as snow
Pure white

As wise as Solomon
Very wise

As wise as an owl
Wise, sensible

To work like a dog

Worked as hard as an Alabama cottonpicker
V

Y,Z

As yellow as a crow's foot
Yellow
As yellow as a guinea
Yellow
As yellow as jaundice
Yellow
As yellow as saffron
Yellow

As yielding as wax
Yielding
As young as dawn
Young
As youthful as the month of May
Young
As zigzag as a lightning
Zigzag in shape

CPSIA information can be obtained
at www.ICGtesting.com
Printed in the USA
LVHW082156100119
603535LV00030B/201/P

9 789350 571484